100 Questions and Answers About Immigrants to the U.S.

Michigan State University
School of Journalism

Read The Spirit Books

an imprint of
David Crumm Media, LLC
Canton, Michigan

For more information and further discussion, visit
news.jrn.msu.edu/culturalcompetence/

Cover art and design by
Rick Nease
www.RickNeaseArt.com

Published By
Read The Spirit Books
an imprint of
David Crumm Media, LLC
42015 Ford Rd., Suite 234
Canton, Michigan, USA

For information about customized editions, bulk
purchases or permissions, contact David Crumm
Media, LLC at info@DavidCrummMedia.com

Contents

Acknowledgments vi

Foreword ix

Preface: Silence is not golden xii

Introduction xiv

Immigrant video stories xxii

Glossary xxiv

Chapter 1: Demographics 1

Chapter 2: History 9

Chapter 3: Immigration process 13

Chapter 4: Health 17

Chapter 5: Assimilation and acculturation 21

Chapter 6: Citizenship 29

Chapter 7: Acceptance 35

Chapter 8: Refugees and asylum seekers 39

Chapter 9: Unauthorized immigrants 42

Chapter 10: Deportation 46

Chapter 11: Families 49

Chapter 12: Work and money 53

Chapter 13: Education 60

Do you know enough to be a citizen? 63

Resources 66

Acknowledgments

The authors of this guide are Michigan State students Jacob Arnold, Sierra Marie Baker, Reagan Dailey-Chwalibog, Juliana Montoya Padilla, David Reiss, Maris Claire Ryckman, Jiayuan Wang and Zixuan Wang. Graphics are by Madeline Carino.

We thank the people who helped edit the guide and ensure its accuracy and credibility. Our expert allies:

Manuel Chavez specializes in international relations, security, crisis communication, democracy and the press. He is an associate professor in the Michigan State University School of Journalism and the director of the Media and Information Studies PhD program at the MSU College of Communication Arts and Sciences.

Angie Chuang is a professor of journalism at American University. She focuses on race and identity issues in news media. In 2000 she developed one of the first regional newspaper race and ethnicity issues beats.

Vincent Delgado is assistant dean for civic engagement in Michigan State University's Residential College in the Arts and Humanities. He is co-founder of Lansing's Refugee Development Center and has been responsible for resettling Afghan families and the Lost Boys of Sudan.

Rana Elmir joined the ACLU of Michigan in 2006 and in 2013 became its deputy director. From Lebanon, Elmir is a graduate of Wayne State University and its Journalism Institute for Minorities.

Molly Hoover's career in international advertising took her to Singapore and Thailand. Her master's thesis at DePaul University was, "Undocumented Migration, the Fourteenth Amendment, and the Enduring Battle Over Who Counts."

Mary Lane is project director at the Kellogg Foundation's Welcome Mat Detroit, part of Global Detroit. She has worked with immigrants and internationals for more than 30 years and studied immigration law at the Detroit College of Law. She also lived as an immigrant in Algeria.

Charles Liu is assistant director at the MSU College of Social Science, Office of Student Affairs and Services. He formerly served as a programming adviser in the MSU Office for International Students and Scholars. Born in Taiwan, he served in the U.S. Marine Corps, earned a law degree from the Ave Maria School of Law and has taught Mandarin Chinese.

Susan Reed has practiced immigration law since 2003 and is managing attorney with the Michigan Immigrant Rights Center. She is a graduate of the University of Minnesota Law School.

Geri Alumit Zeldes is an associate professor in the MSU School of Journalism. She is a professor and documentary filmmaker and a recipient of MSU's Excellence in Diversity Award for "Advancing Global Competency." This publication follows a guide for journalists created by Zeldes and her students in 2010. Two of those students, **Jennifer Orlando** and **Joy (Walter) Shantz**, helped edit this guide.

The **Pew Research Center** has helped on many guides in this series. For this one, Pew's **Mark Hugo Lopez, Ana Gonzalez-Barrera** and **Jens Manuel Krogstad** gave advice in advance of the class and then reviewed a draft of the guide.

We thank **Lucinda Davenport**, professor and director of the MSU College of Communication Arts and Sciences' School of Journalism for her continuing support of this series.

Foreword

By Sonia Nazario

Immigration is among the most contentious issues in the United States. When I speak about this issue around the country, some colleges hire extra security guards. Still, consistently, six in 10 Americans say they would allow immigrants who came to this country unlawfully to have some path to legalize.

Why the gap between the rhetoric and reality? Immigrants used to mostly settle in six states: California, New York, Texas, California, Florida and Illinois. Most people in this country didn't personally know an immigrant. Many still don't.

Their view of immigrants came from an increasingly polarized media—where people who are conservative watch TV channels that confirm their views and biases, and people who are liberal watch other channels that do the same.

In the past two decades, migrants have spread out. In search of jobs, they have gone to every nook and cranny of this country: to meatpacking plants in Omaha, Nebraska, construction sites to re-build New Orleans after Hurricane Katrina, poultry processing lines in Pocahontas, Arkansas.

People have gotten to know an immigrant as someone who cleans their offices at night, mows their lawn, takes care of their children. They no longer see them as a black-and-white caricature: the criminal rapist hell-bent on taking jobs from Americans who will destroy the country, or the saintly worker whose hard work and sacrifice will cure all that ails the U.S. economy. They see that immigrant not as a one-dimensional saint or sinner—but as a human being. They begin to empathize with immigrant struggles.

Ultimately, this is what will alter the discussion about immigrants: Facts provided by this book, to dispel the many myths I hear around the country about immigrants, and a personal connection to one immigrant and their story.

Empathy is needed more now than ever. Most migrants coming to the U.S. unlawfully today aren't coming from Mexico for a better economic life. Most are coming from Central America. They are fleeing some of the most dangerous countries on Earth— where control by gangs and narco traffickers bringing drugs from Latin America to the U.S. means children as young as 9 or 10 in Honduras are recruited by these bad actors to work for them. If you refuse, they kill you.

They are refugees.

In my travels in the U.S. and in Central America, I have met many of these children. I urge readers of this book to meet one of these children in your community.

If you do, you will see someone with strengths and flaws, someone looking for safety, freedom and opportunity.

Someone not so different from ourselves.

Sonia Nazario is an award-winning journalist and author who has written about immigration, hunger and drug addiction. Her book "Enrique's Journey" traces the life of a boy who fled Honduras to be reunited with his mother in the United States. A fluent Spanish speaker of Jewish ancestry, Nazario has lived in Argentina and followed Enrique's route.

Preface: Silence is not golden

By Bing Goei

Immigration has been one of our nation's most effective tools in establishing America as the greatest nation in the world. Immigrants have made many contributions to develop a U.S. economy that is second to none. Immigrants have added to the rich and diverse cultures of this great nation. Immigrants from all around the world have arrived on our shores and have been able to find a new life filled with hope and opportunities. Why then is the Asian immigrants' story so unknown? Why then have the Asian immigrants' many needs not been addressed? The answer is: silence. My silence. Your silence. Our silence.

The decision my parents made to flee Indonesia during the reign of President Sukarno was a decision that I could not understand as a 6-year-old boy. What I do know now is that my parents made the sacrifice for the benefit of their children. I also recognize and acknowledge that this sacrifice has been repeated by many parents and has benefitted many of their children and their children's children.

I will never forget my parents' sacrifice and it has instilled in me the responsibility to ensure that I must continue to live out their values by lifting up other immigrants who need a hand up or a voice to advocate for their constitutional right to life, liberty and the pursuit of happiness.

Many of us have been able to live the American dream in our adopted country. Many of us are enjoying a quality of life that we would not have been able to provide for our children and grandchildren if we did not live in this great country called America. With these blessings, we now must accept the responsibility to share our stories and to be the voice for those who have no voice within our communities.

> *"In the end, we will remember not the words of our enemies, but the silence of our friends."*
> —*Martin Luther King Jr.*

Bing Goei is director of the Michigan Office for New Americans, a community leader and entrepreneur. He immigrated to West Michigan from Indonesia, by way of the Netherlands, in 1960.

Introduction

Over the years, U.S. immigration policies and issues have cycled—surging and subsiding during different periods. In 2016, fueled by U.S. presidential politics, immigration reform moved to the forefront—with a lot at stake. Defining their campaign platforms, candidates placed a spotlight on these issues—often citing statistics that are misleading or inaccurate. To be certain, some data are difficult to obtain and must be extrapolated using other measures.

Issues at the heart of immigration policy and Americans' perspectives about it are formed by complex political, socio-economic, workplace, human safety, assimilation, citizenship, and resettlement issues, among others. These factors are informed by data and trends surrounding demographics, employment, resource allocation, taxes, crime statistics, and so on. Through data balanced with interviews from immigrants to the United States, we hope to provide quantitative and qualitative insights into some of these issues in this book. The aim of this book, then, with help from experts in the field, is to provide factual insight into the "hard" and "soft" interpretations of underlying issues. Information is power—BUT having accurate information is key.

The United States is frequently referred to as a "nation of immigrants," yet some of the data and information seem to be paradoxical. Writing for The American Interest, Peter Feinman, president of the research-based Institute of History, Archaeology and Education, reviewed 2013 UN statistics. They indicate the United States admits the largest number of immigrants in the world, yet, at 13.3 percent, ranked 68th out of 231 countries in its percentage of immigrant population in 2015. Not knowing or comprehending the relative position of the United States in global migration patterns has contributed to skepticism about U.S. immigration policy and to proposals for more restrictive policies. Patterns of skepticism are evident throughout U.S. history— even going back to our founding fathers. In 1751, Ben Franklin wrote in Observations Concerning the Increase of Mankind, Peopling the Countries, etc.:

> *Why should Pennsylvania, founded by the English, become a Colony of Aliens, who will shortly be so numerous as to Germanize us, instead of our Anglicifying them, and will never adopt our language or customs any more than they can acquire our complexion?"*

Is it surprising, then, that immigration headlined the 2016 campaign? The authors and contributors hope "100 Questions and Answers About Immigrants to the U.S." helps inform conversations on this critical topic.

View video at:
https://www.youtube.com/
watch?v=jrB0otm2VRo

Is being a U.S. citizen the same as being an American?

Being a U.S. citizen implies a legal status and affords certain rights. Drawing from the Constitution, the Department of Homeland Security outlines the stipulations. Citizenship can happen at birth or after. To be a citizen by birth, an individual must be born in the United States or "certain territories or outlying possessions of the United States, and subject to the jurisdiction of the United States" or have a parent(s) who is/are citizens when he/she was born. To become a citizen after birth, one must "apply for 'derived' or 'acquired' citizenship through parents or through the naturalization process for foreign citizens or nationals."

Current U.S. citizenship policies, however, do not reflect past policies. Historically, in some immigration waves to the United States, citizenship wasn't even offered to immigrants or individuals born in the United States. Examples include Blacks and African Americans, Native Americans, Chinese, and others. Akbar Amed, chair of Islamic Studies at American University, raised the legal aspects of citizenship and the foundational rights bestowed under the Constitution and the commitment to these principles. For The Huffington Post, he wrote, "Being a legal citizen is more than the acquisition of a passport, it is also the recognition of the ideas that were forged by the Founding Fathers of the United States ... George Washington, Thomas Jefferson, James Madison, and Benjamin Franklin."

"Being an American" is different. Answers to the question of who is an American will likely depend on whom you ask. In The Atlantic, journalist Karina Martinez-Carter wrote that U.S. citizens equate self-identification as "an American" with being a U.S. citizen. She suggested that citizens of Latin America say they, too, are "American" likely because they live in an American continent. Europeans will probably say that an American is someone from the U.S.A. Perceptions vary because U.S. citizens have claimed "American" as a nationality despite the fact the Americas include many countries.

American cultural traditions

Given the imprecision of who or what is "American," let's tackle the cultural dimensions of Americanism. Again, there are many views. It is analogous to taking U.S. students to study abroad. They might describe the people they meet as being "very different from us in the U.S.," not realizing they formed this impression in reference to their own culture. Regardless of how deeply they understand that new culture, what they are expressing is "they are different from me" with little understanding that they hold their own cultural stereotypes.

Given all these factors, is there just one American culture? The consensus seems to be that there is not. As a "nation of immigrants," then, one could say that immigrants have helped shape American culture. Because of this, the United States has been described as a "melting pot," reflecting the multitude of cultures in the country. More recently, the cultural description has shifted to a "salad bowl" analogy, reflecting pluralistic values and the co-existence of individual cultures. Critics of this analogy say the United States should have one common culture. Countering this is the notion that it is possible for individuals to adapt to a new culture without abandoning the heritages into which they were born.

An important element of cultural conformity is language. Although most people in the United States speak English, the U.S. Census Bureau reports 382 languages and language groups in the country. Some legislators have proposed that English should be designated as the official national language in the United States, but no legislation has passed. West Virginia has made English its official language and similar legislation has been introduced in other states.

What about race and ethnicity in the U.S.?

Different interpretations of race and ethnicity and their use in statistics contribute to misunderstandings about immigrants and immigration policy. What is the difference between race and ethnic background or ethnicity? Fundamentally, race is thought of as a social construct based on biological or physical features such as skin and eye color. Ethnicity, however, is socio-culturally determined and includes ancestry, nationality, regional culture and language. Sociologist Dalton Conley adds, "You can identify ethnically as Irish and Polish, but you have to be essentially either black or white. The fundamental difference is that race is socially imposed and hierarchical." On PBS' "Race - The Power of an Illusion," John Cheng wrote, "… the most powerful argument about the differentiation between race and ethnicity is that race becomes institutionalized in a way that has profound social consequences on the members of different groups." Distinctions between race and ethnicity have changed over time, which has led to confusion and overlap.

Criticisms abound that the U.S. Census Bureau has contributed to misunderstandings about race and ethnicity and that the Census does not accurately reflect the increasing diversity of the U.S. population. The federal Office of Management and Budget mandates the race categories used in the Census and has changed its treatment of race and ethnicity. The office announced that "racial and ethnic categories set forth in the standards should not be interpreted as being primarily biological or genetic in reference. Race and ethnicity may be thought of in terms of social and cultural characteristics as well as ancestry." Inaccuracy of race, ethnicity and nationality identification when gathering and interpreting data can contribute to misunderstanding and inaccurate stereotypes about immigrant subpopulations.

Immigrants in the work force

At the center of the immigration debate is the perception that immigrants take jobs from citizens. Recent studies suggest this is not the case. In a 2015 paper for the National Bureau of Economic Research, Gihoon Hong and John McLaren reported their analysis of 1980-2000 U.S. Census data. According to their report, one immigrant to the United States actually creates 1.2 jobs, which are generally taken by native-born citizens. "Immigrants appear to raise local non-tradable ('hospitality, teaching, retail and construction') sector wages and to attract native-born workers from elsewhere in the country," they wrote. "Overall, it appears that local workers benefit from the arrival of more immigrants."

According to a study by the Stanford Latino Entrepreneurship Initiative, net new business creation among Latinos grew 47 percent in 2007-2012. At the same time, non-Latino new business development decreased by 2 percent. Henry Cisneros, secretary of Housing and Urban Development under President Bill Clinton, and Sol Trujillo, chairman of the Latino Donor Collaborative, wrote about the study in a Wall Street Journal commentary. They wrote that, compared with the general population, Latinos in the United States are younger, better educated and have higher earning power. As the general population ages and retires, this group will contribute to a stronger workforce. Similarly, government statistics indicate "every million new immigrants will pay $500 billion more into the Social Security Trust Fund over 25 years than they will take out."

This guide takes up these and many other topics associated with immigrants and immigration. The answers build on each other, showing the complexity and interrelatedness of these topics. We hope this guide answers some of your questions.

Dawn Thorndike Pysarchik
Guide editor
Professor, Department of Advertising + Public Relations
Michigan State University

Joe Grimm
Series editor
School of Journalism
Michigan State University

Immigrant video stories

A stew of statistics does not describe immigrant experiences. To really understand immigrants, you need to know some individual stories. The Immigration History Research Center at the University of Minnesota, founded in 1965, works to convey how people understand immigration in the past and present. The center is the oldest and largest interdisciplinary research center and archives about immigrant and refugee life in North America. Since 2013, the center's Immigrant Stories project has trained immigrants, refugees and their family members to make short videos to preserve and share experiences of the United States' most recent immigrants.

Immigrant Stories Project Manager Elizabeth Venditto helped bring stories to this guide.

According to the Immigrant Stories website, "We chose digital storytelling as our methodology because it allows migrants to determine both the form and content of their stories. Participants respond to a broad prompt to 'Tell us your immigrant story.' We encourage them to recount a story that they feel comfortable sharing publicly and that they would most like preserved for future generations. ... Our collection contains stories from first-generation immigrants and refugees (that is, people born outside the United States) as well as stories created by their children and grandchildren."

We encourage you to follow the links throughout the guide to watch some of the more than 165 Immigrant Stories collected by the center. You can learn about the project at immigrantstories.umn.edu. Click "watch stories" to see them.

Immigrant Stories are shared under a Creative Commons Attribution-NonCommercial 4.0 International License. The project received funding from the University of Minnesota, John S. and James L. Knight Foundation, the Digital Public Library of America, and the National Endowment for the Humanities.

Glossary

adjustment of status: Federal regulation permits change of individuals' immigration status while in the United States.

alien: U.S. law says an alien is someone who is not a citizen or national of the country. This guide usually uses more precise terms such as legal immigrant, unauthorized immigrant or legal permanent resident.

asylum: This is protection that a country offers people who are unable or unwilling to return to their home country because of persecution or fear of persecution. A person who has or who is seeking asylum is an asylee. Asylum is defined under international law.

citizen: Someone who has the legal right to be in the country and has the privileges and protection of that country.

DACA: Deferred Action for Childhood Arrivals.

DAPA: Deferred Action for Parents of Americans and Lawful Permanent Residents.

emigrate: Often confused with **immigrate,** the difference is in perspective. "Emigrate" refers to individuals moving out of their country to live in another. "Immigrate" means moving into a new country. From the U.S. perspective, one would say someone "emigrated from the United States to another country" or someone "immigrated into the United States."

expatriate: A noun or a verb, it refers to people who have voluntarily left their home country to live and work in another country. Expat for short.

green card: This is the common name for the Permanent Resident Card, also known as Form I-551. It is actually blue, not green. It is issued as evidence of lawful permanent resident status in the United States. Most Permanent Resident Cards are valid for 10 years, though some have no expiration date. Green-card holders are immigrants.

ICE: U.S. Immigration and Customs Enforcement is part of the Department of Homeland Security. It succeeded the Immigration and Naturalization Service in 2003. Its job is to enforce federal laws covering border control, customs, trade and immigration.

migrate: To move from one place to another. People can migrate within a country.

nativism: The policy or belief that favors the interests of a country's native or naturalized citizens above the interests of immigrants.

nonimmigrant: Someone admitted to a country for a specific period of time with clear conditions. Classifications include: foreign government officials, visitors for business or pleasure, students, temporary workers and many others. Most can be accompanied or joined by spouses and unmarried minor or dependent children.

naturalize: The legal action of a government to grant citizenship to someone from another country.

permanent residency: This visa status allows someone to live and work indefinitely in a country where they are not a citizen. This can be a step toward citizenship.

quotas: Annual limits on immigrants are set by U.S. law. There are country quotas and an overall cap.

refugee: Someone fleeing their home country because of a fear of persecution based upon race, membership in a social group, political opinion, religion, national origin or sexual orientation. Refugees are described under international law, just as asylum is.

visa: Permission to enter a country, temporarily stay in it, or leave. Visas usually are placed in the passports or travel documents issued by the original country. Visas may either allow or prohibit working privileges.

xenophobia: Unreasonable fear or hatred of people from other countries or foreigners.

Demographics

1 How many immigrants are there in the United States?

There were more than 42.4 million, 13.3 percent of the U.S. population, in 2014, according to the Census Bureau's American Community Survey. Immigrants and their U.S.-born children now equal about 81 million, about one fourth of the nation's 325 million people.

2 How many immigrants arrive legally in the United States each year?

According to the Census Bureau, 1.3 million foreign-born people moved to the United States in 2014. That was up 11 percent from 1.2 million in 2013. The leading countries of origin were India, 147,500; China, 131,800; Mexico, 130,000; Canada, 41,200, and the Philippines with 40,500.

3 Are there limits on how many people can come from specific countries?

Yes, there are country quotas. The Immigration and Naturalization Act of 1965 refocused immigration on family reunification and attracting skilled labor. The previous system was based on country of origin. This shifted policy from favoring Europe and allows more immigration from Latin American, Asia and Africa.

4 Who sets immigration numbers?

The permanent immigrant allocation is set by the Immigration and Naturalization Act. There are limits on certain groups of immigrants, such as those joining family members who are citizens or those on work visas. According to the American Immigration Council, currently no more than 7 percent of total immigration annually can come from an individual country. Refugee admission numbers and allocations change based on world circumstances and are set annually by the president and Congress.

5 Where are U.S. immigrants from?

According to the Migration Policy Institute, these were the top 10 countries of origin in 2014:

Mexico	28 percent
India	5 percent
China	5 percent
The Philippines	4 percent

What's the immigrant composition?

The immigration population is changing. Currently, the majority of immigrants come form Hispanic countries, but in the next 50 years that will shift to Asia.

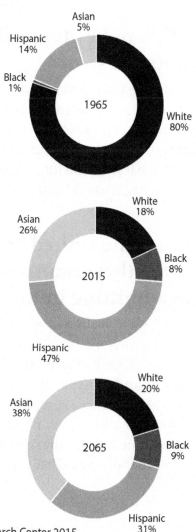

Asian
5%

Hispanic
14%

Black
1%

1965

White
80%

White
18%

Asian
26%

Black
8%

2015

Hispanic
47%

White
20%

Asian
38%

Black
9%

2065

Hispanic
31%

Source: Pew Research Center 2015
Illustration: Madeline Carino

Vietnam	3 percent
El Salvador	3 percent
Cuba	3 percent
South Korea	3 percent
Dominican Republic	2 percent
Guatemala	2 percent

6 Does U.S. policy treat all immigrants the same?

Since the 1600s, the United States has accepted immigration applications from countries around the world. In practice, however, exceptions create an uneven playing field. Refugees and asylum seekers are considered separately. Asylum seekers may apply at ports of entry. There is no limit on asylees.

7 How does the United States compare to other countries in regard to admitting immigrants?

According to a United Nations report for 2013, the United States admitted more immigrants than any other country, followed by Germany, the United Kingdom, France and Canada. The United States' 70,000 allowance for refugee resettlements also was the largest. However with a total population of more than 300 million, the immigrant share of the U.S. population was 13.3 percent. That was 68th in the world.

8 Why do people want to immigrate to the United States?

Immigration is difficult and not always guaranteed, so people have various reasons for wanting to be here. Major reasons are to reunite their families, for economic opportunity and for safety.

9 How important is family reunification in immigration?

It can be so important that people risk their lives. The 1965 Immigration and Nationality Act made family unification and skilled labor the top criteria for admitting immigrants to the United States. The desire to be with family can also pull people back to their countries of origin.

10 Where do U.S. immigrants settle?

Since the 2000 census, immigrants have been more likely to settle in urban areas. This mirrors settlement patterns from the1800s and follows today's general population pattern in the country. The two largest immigrant groups are Hispanics and Asians. In 2013, 46 percent were Hispanic or Latino, and 26 percent identified as Asian. By region, Hispanic and Latino immigrants have traditionally settled in the greatest numbers in the Southwest and more recently in the Pacific Northwest. More than half of Asian immigrants live in California, New York,

Texas, New Jersey and Hawaii, according to the U.S. Census Bureau. It reported that the top 10 cities for immigrants in 2013 were Miami, San Jose, Los Angeles, San Francisco, New York, San Diego, Houston, Washington, D.C., Las Vegas and Riverside, California.

11 Do Americans emigrate to other countries?

U.S. emigration is at a record high and climbing but is tiny compared with the numbers of people immigrating into the United States. The U.S. Treasury Department keeps track of those who renounce their citizenship or terminate long-term U.S. residency. These Treasury Department numbers for recent years are minimums:

2012	932
2013	2,999
2014	3,415
2015	4,279

However, the number who migrate to other countries without renouncing their citizen is quite large. Estimates about the number of Americans living overseas vary, but are around 8 million with about 2.5 million of them in Mexico. Concerns that people emigrate out of the United States to escape taxes have prompted laws to capture some of that money.

Where do immigrants live?

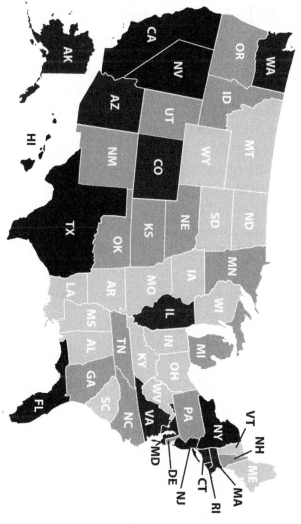

Number of immigrants by state

- < 5%
- 5 - 9.9%
- 10 - 14.9%
- > 15%

States containing the most immigrants

1. California
2. New York
3. Texas
4. Florida
5. New Jersey
6. Illinois
7. Massachusetts
8. Georgia
9. Virginia
10. Washington

Illustration: Madeline Carino
Source: U.S. Census Bureau, 2010 American Community Survey

12 What are the predominant religions of U.S. immigrants?

The predominant religion of authorized immigrants in the United States is Christianity. That declined from 78.4 percent to 70.6 percent between 2007 and 2014, according to the Pew Research Center. In the same period, those who were not affiliated with any religion increased from 16.1 percent to 22.8. The portion of immigrants who are Muslim increased from 0.4 percent to 0.9 percent and Hindus increased from 0.4 percent to 0.7 percent. Most Christian immigrants are from Latin America.

History

13 Have motivations for immigration changed over the years?

In the 18th and 19th centuries, economic factors were major drivers of immigration. These included fleeing hard times and attraction to jobs in the United States. In the late 20th century, however, following changes in U.S. policy, a better living environment and family reunification became more important. Recently, new immigrants pursue high-skilled work, education, quality of life and higher social status.

14 How has U.S. immigration policy changed in recent years?

Major changes include:

1962: The Migration and Refugee Assistance Act addressed the unanticipated need to help refugees, displaced persons, conflict victims and others at risk.

1965: The Immigration and Naturalization Act replaced country quotas that favored Europeans with preferences for skills and family reunification. This opened immigration from many more countries.

1980: The United States Refugee Act of 1980 provided a permanent system for admission and resettlement for people covered by the 1962 and 1965 acts.

1986: The Immigration Reform and Control Act focused on border control and the legalization of unauthorized immigrants who met certain requirements. It legalized some kinds of seasonal agricultural workers. It also legalized unauthorized immigrants with conditions. They had to have resided here since Jan. 1, 1982; have at least minimal knowledge of U.S. history, government and English; and not be guilty of crimes.

2012: President Barack Obama announced the Deferred Action for Childhood Arrivals. This was meant to provide deportation relief and work opportunities for unauthorized adults who came to this country before their 16th birthday and before June 2007.

2014: Obama provided similar benefits to the unauthorized immigrant parents of U.S.-born children. This was called the Deferred Action for Parents of Americans and Lawful Permanent Residents. This plan also expanded the 2012 DACA program.

2016: On a 4-4 vote, the U.S. Supreme Court let stand a lower court decision blocking Obama's 2014 program. The Migration Policy Institute estimated that more than 10 million people live in households with people eligible under Deferred Action for Parents of Americans.

15 How have immigration numbers grown in recent years?

According to a Migration Policy Institute analysis of U.S. Census and American Community Survey data, the increase looks like this:

Year	Immigrants	Percent of population
1970	9.6 million	4.7
1980	14.1 million	6.2
1990	19.8 million	7.9
2000	31.3 million	11.1
2010	40.0 million	12.9
2014	42.4 million	13.3

16 What is the historic significance of Ellis Island?

Located in New York Harbor within sight of the Statue of Liberty, this was a key immigration point into the United States. From 1892 to 1954, more than 12 million immigrants were admitted at Ellis Island. When they arrived, they were identified from vessel documentation and received legal and medical inspections. In 1976, the island re-opened as a historic site. San Francisco Bay's Angel Island, known as "the Ellis Island of the West," operated from 1920 to 1940. It admitted about a million people from China, Japan and 80 other countries. Because Angel Island included a detention or holding center, it has a more somber story than Ellis Island.

17 What's the most common entry point for immigrants today?

For legal immigrants, the most common entry point is New York City, and the busiest airport is New York's JFK International, according to the U.S. Customs and Border Patrol. For unauthorized immigrants, the Texas border is most common.

18 Is it true that Mexican immigrants are returning to Mexico?

Since the 2007-2009 recession, more Mexicans have left the United States than have come in. The Pew Research Center discovered this by comparing two numbers. One is from the Mexican National Survey of Demographic Dynamics, which showed that one million people returned to Mexico from the United States between 2009 and 2014. The second number, from the U.S. Census, showed 870,000 people coming into the United States from Mexico during that period. The result was a net decline of 130,000 people. Reasons included border enforcement and declining economic opportunity in the United States. Most people returning to Mexico did so on their own, usually to be with their families.

Immigration process

19 Is everyone with a visa an immigrant?

No. There are immigrant and nonimmigrant visas.
Immigrant visas are issued to individuals who will
live in the United States permanently. Nonimmigrant
visas are for people who wish to be in the United
States temporarily, usually for work, study or
travel. They have expiration dates. People with
temporary visas are not immigrants. According
to U.S. federal agencies, in 2015 about 45 million
people came to the United States on nonimmigrant
visas. One million people came hoping to immigrate
permanently.

20 How many types of visas are there?

There are about as many kinds of visas as there
are countries in the world: around 200. There
are immigrant visas and more than 30 types of
nonimmigrant visas for workers, students, tourists

and victims of violence. There are many kinds of work visas, as the United States uses the program to select workers from the global employment pool. There are specific visas for superior athletes and entertainers, and visas for people fleeing danger or human trafficking. Since the 1990s, investors who put $500,000 into a "Regional Center" and who pledge to create or preserve 10 jobs can qualify for an EB-5 permanent resident visa. A Regional Center is an organization designated by the U. S. Citizenship and Immigration Services for investment.

21 Why don't people just wait instead of immigrating illegally?

Some people feel an urgency to immigrate, and the wait can be very long. According to the Migration Policy Institute, in April 2016, the federal government was still processing some family-sponsored visa applications dating back almost 24 years. Some employment-related visa applications dated back almost 12 years. Many people are not eligible for any legal immigration program. There is no "line" to get in and no amount of waiting that could result in lawful admission.

22 Are there immigration watch lists?

Yes. The U.S. government places individuals on lists for national security or political reasons. Relationships between certain countries and the United States can also mean higher scrutiny.

23 Which U.S. agencies are in charge of immigration?

Three agencies of the Department of Homeland Security oversee immigration policy, investigation and enforcement:

- U.S. Customs and Border Protection monitors the borders with the U.S. Border Patrol. It directly patrols international land borders, apprehending people who are trying to enter illegally or smuggle others in.
- U.S. Immigration and Customs Enforcement enforces immigration laws within the United States. It investigates, arrests, detains and removes people living in the United States illegally.
- U.S. Citizenship and Immigration Services reviews and grants immigrant applications and decides who receives citizenship.

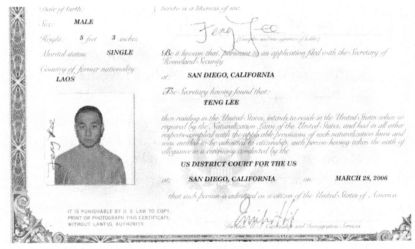

Teng Lee's family members were refugees who fled to Thailand after the communist takeover of Laos. Teng was born in a refugee camp in Thailand. His family came to the United States with a bag of immigration documents. View video at: http://immigrants.mndigital.org/items/show/513

Health

24 Must immigrants pass health tests to be admitted?

The Centers for Disease Control and Prevention has set health requirements. They include a "physical examination, mental health evaluation, syphilis serologic testing, review of vaccination records, and chest radiography, followed by acid-fast bacillus smears and sputum cultures if the chest radiograph suggests tuberculosis." The examinations check for mental and physical diseases that could harm others. Treatment for conditions such as tuberculosis and certain sexually transmitted diseases is required before immigration.

25 Must immigrants receive immunizations to enter the country?

If someone cannot prove they have received vaccinations, they will get them at the exam. Vaccinations are based on age, potential danger or diseases that are no longer a problem in the United States. Nonimmigrant visitors typically do not undergo health screening.

26 Does it matter what country people are coming from?

The prevalence of certain diseases or conditions in the home country is weighed in the examination process.

27 Do immigrants bring diseases into the country?

This has been claimed in political campaigns, but there have not been large outbreaks. According to the U.S. Centers for Disease Control and Prevention, "The sheer number of people who live, work, and travel between the United States and Mexico has led to a sharing of culture and commerce, as well as the easy transportation of infectious diseases." The United States and Mexico work jointly, the CDC reports, to "detect, notify, investigate, and respond to illness reports and communicable disease cases."

28 Do unauthorized immigrants burden the health system?

The policy journal Health Affairs reported that, on a per-person basis, "the cost of providing health care to immigrants is lower than that of providing care to U.S. natives." It further said, "immigrants are not contributing disproportionately to high health-care costs in public programs such as Medicaid." A 2015 article in the Journal of General Internal Medicine suggested that undocumented immigrants did not burden the system but actually provided $35.1 billion in surplus payments to the Medicare Trust Fund between 2000 and 2011. Many unauthorized immigrants do not seek medical services for fear of being apprehended and deported.

29 What is the "healthy immigrant effect"?

This is the phenomenon of immigrants who arrive in good health and who get worse after they arrive in the United States. This could be because of new stresses or adapting to a lifestyle with less exercise and healthy foods. It has been suggested that the effect might simply be a matter of better health care detecting previously unknown health conditions.

My Journey to Refuge

Caceelia Moe was born in Chumphon, Thailand, in 1991. Her family moved to Mawker refugee camp in Thailand in 1992 and another refugee camp in 1999. Her family was resettled to St. Paul, Minnesota, in 2001. View video at: http://immigrants.mndigital.org/items/show/652

Assimilation and acculturation

30 What is the difference between assimilation and acculturation?

Assimilation is when a person or group's language and culture become similar to that of the place they are assimilating into. Acculturation is a cultural exchange in which, through contact with each other, groups exchange cultural ways and become a little more alike. Assimilation is seen as being absorbed and losing one's original culture. Acculturation is seen as keeping the original culture and adding to it. The difference has social, anthropological and political meanings.

31 Do most immigrants want to become part of American culture?

Many immigrants want to be part of their new country without losing their home culture. This can mean learning the dominant language, customs, values, behaviors and traditions. Most immigrants recognize that the faster they assimilate, the better their chances for upward mobility.

32 Are immigrants loyal to their home country or the United States?

People can be loyal to both. They may still have strong feelings for and family in their previous country, but that does not imply a lack of loyalty to their new country. People who become U.S. citizens take this oath of allegiance:

> *I hereby declare, on oath, that I absolutely and entirely renounce and abjure all allegiance and fidelity to any foreign prince, potentate, state, or sovereignty, of whom or which I have heretofore been a subject or citizen; that I will support and defend the Constitution and laws of the United States of America against all enemies, foreign and domestic; that I will bear true faith and allegiance to the same; that I will bear arms on behalf of the United States when required by the law; that I will perform noncombatant service in the Armed Forces of the United States when required by the law; that I will perform work of national importance under civilian direction when required by the law; and that I take this obligation freely, without any mental reservation or purpose of evasion; so help me God.*

33 Why don't today's immigrants assimilate as quickly as previous generations did?

Actually, recent immigrants are assimilating faster, according to the National Academies of Sciences, Engineering and Medicine. The Manhattan Institute reported in 2013 that immigrants assimilated faster than at any point since the 1980s. This is because they are more skilled and educated than previous generations. More second-generation immigrants are also acquiring English language proficiency to a greater degree than before, although a side effect is that more also lose their native language.

34 What factors help immigrants assimilate?

Higher income, English proficiency and working with others can help. Being married or having children also helps, as this can lead to interactions with other people, parents and teachers. Community and church activities also help. Everyday interactions at work provide more opportunities to learn American ways.

35 What does first- and second-generation mean?

First-generation immigrants are people who immigrate to a new country. Second-generation

immigrants are their children. Third-generation
immigrants are the children of second-generation
immigrants. The 1.5 generation or 1.5G refers to
someone who immigrated before or during their
early teens. According to a Pew Research Center
report, of the approximately 234.7 million U.S. adults,
37.4 million are first-generation, 19.7 million are
second-generation and 177.7 million are third or
higher.

36 What are initial challenges for immigrants?

Early priorities are finding a job and learning
English. Those who arrive with both have an easier
start. Recently, immigrants have arrived with higher
education levels, which has helped them adapt,
although English writing skills are often better
than conversational skills. It may be more difficult
for older immigrants to adapt than younger ones
because of cultural conflicts. If immigrants come
to the United States alone and don't know anybody,
homesickness can be a challenge. This can be
especially so for those in close-knit families.

37 Do immigrants know English when they arrive?

Many do, especially those from countries where
English is widely used. These countries include
Canada, Jamaica, the United Kingdom, India,
Nigeria and the Philippines. English is common

in countries once ruled by the British. A 2013 Migration Policy Institute report states that more than half the immigrants in the United States speak English "very well."

38 Is there a correlation between education and adjusting?

Researchers measure assimilation in three ways: economic, cultural and civil. Education can help in all three areas. Education can improve employment chances and helps people learn, which is key to culture and learning about language, laws and government.

39 What programs help immigrants learn English?

These are called English as a Second Language or English to Speakers of Other Languages classes. Community colleges, churches, local community groups, libraries and school districts offer them. Classes are typically small. They teach reading, writing and spoken fluency. Most are publicly funded. Often the learners in such classes have different native languages and together study vocabulary, grammar, communication and civics.

40 Do accents affect assimilation?

Accent discrimination at work rose by 76 percent from 1997 to 2011, according to the U.S. Equal

Employment Opportunity Commission. An employer can refuse to hire or promote someone to a position that requires proficient and clear English. Immigrants with accents may be inhibited about freely expressing themselves or can be misunderstood. Some immigrants take classes to lose their accents.

41 What are "English only" laws?

This means adopting English as the country's official language. "English only" or "official English" initiatives have occurred since the 1700s to discourage German, French or Spanish and some indigenous languages. According to the website ProEnglish, which prefers the term "official English," "Having English as our official language simply means that for the government to act officially, or legally, it must communicate in English. It means the language of record is the English language, and that no one has a right to demand government services in any other language." Opponents say official English would reduce multilingualism and demean and discourage people whose native language is not English.

42 Do immigrants' views of their original country change?

Many immigrants have relatives and friends in their home countries, so they stay in touch and follow the news there. Some immigrants who visit their home countries have been surprised or disappointed to see that things have changed. Others note that immigrants sometimes try to maintain their culture in the United States in ways that become outdated in their home countries.

43 Where do immigrants stand on deportation and citizenship?

The Pew Research Center's Hispanic Trends project asked Hispanic and Asian immigrants about these top immigration issues in 2013. Both groups said that reducing deportations is more important to them than creating a pathway to citizenship.

44 How do U.S. immigrants feel about the future?

Several studies give indications. A 2016 report by the Pew Research Center said that U.S. Hispanics are more optimistic than the general population about their finances and their children's economic mobility. However, they expressed concern about the rising cost of living. In 2014, a W.K. Kellogg Foundation study of 1,000 Latino adult immigrants stated they were more optimistic than those born in the United States. Immigrants were hopeful about new possibilities, while people born here were concerned about continuing inequality, or declining opportunities. Furthermore, a 2014 Pew study reported that U.S. citizens are generally more optimistic than people in other countries. The study attributed that to an influx of immigrants who have helped slow the aging of the United States.

Liang Xiong, who is Hmong, lived in the Chiang Kham Refugee Camp in Thailand and came to the United States in 1987, though she had many relatives still living in Laos. View video at: http://immigrants.mndigital.org/items/show/491

Citizenship

45 Do most immigrants to the United States become citizens?

A 2013 Pew report said Census records showed 36 percent of the 5.4 million legal immigrants from Mexico had become citizens, compared with 68 percent of non-Mexican legal immigrants. Influences can include personal factors, finances, language, ability to pass the citizenship exam, proximity to home country and how U.S. citizenship would affect native citizenship. According to U.S. Citizenship and Immigration Services, every year about 680,000 people become citizens during naturalization ceremonies across the United States and around the world. The Immigration and Naturalization Act allows a ceiling of 675,000 permanent immigrants annually, plus additional close family members. Although these numbers are similar, there are thousands more who immigrate in different ways and thousands who chose to remain as legal permanent residents, without citizenship.

46 How does an immigrant become a U.S. citizen?

There are several steps. The first step is to establish eligibility. Generally, this is done by being a permanent resident who lives in the United States for at least five years. After the application, there is a background check and fingerprinting. Then, there is an interview with U.S Citizenship and Immigration Services and English and civics testing. Applications may either be granted, continued or denied. Approvals can take an average of six months or as much time as Immigration Services says is needed.

47 How much does it cost to apply for citizenship?

Application fees are $680 per person, which includes $595 for the application and $85 for the background check and fingerprinting. Each family member must pay, and fees are not refundable. Legal costs paid to lawyers are additional.

48 How do U.S. citizenship requirements compare to others?

The financial website Investopedia ranks the United States as one of the world's five toughest countries in which to gain citizenship. The others are Austria, Germany, Japan and Switzerland. Other lists by immigration law firms and publications mention North Korea, China, Mexico, Bhutan, the United

Arab Emirates, Finland and The Vatican as difficult for citizenship.

49 What is dual citizenship?

Dual citizens have the rights and obligations of two countries. The U.S. Supreme Court sanctioned dual citizenship in 1967. The United States allows immigrants who naturalize to keep their original citizenship. It also allows Americans who become citizens of other countries to remain U.S. citizens. However, scores of countries do not allow people to keep their native citizenships there if they become naturalized Americans. Scores of other countries do. The country of residence has the upper hand when there are conflicts. The U.S. Department of State discourages dual citizenship.

50 What is a legal permanent resident?

A legal permanent resident is an immigrant who is not a citizen, but who can stay and work indefinitely. They are on a Form I-551, a so-called "green card." The paths to permanent residence typically have to do with work or family. People can jeopardize chances for permanent residency status and be deported or barred from re-entry if they leave the country for extended periods or falsely claim to be citizens. United States Citizenship and Immigration Services said there were 13.3 million legal permanent residents on Jan. 1, 2012. About 8.8 million were eligible to naturalize.

51 What is a resident alien?

This is the former term for permanent resident. Permanent resident cards used to be called "alien registration cards."

52 Can immigrants vote?

Yes, as long as the immigrant is 18 years or older and a citizen. Naturalized citizens vote more than natural-born citizens. Permanent residents may not vote in federal elections. According to the Pew Research Center in 2016, "Hispanics and Asians have long had significantly lower voter turnout rates than whites and blacks. Hispanics and Asians who are naturalized citizens tend to have higher voter turnout rates than their U.S.-born counterparts. In 2012, naturalized-immigrant Hispanics had a voter turnout rate of 54 percent, compared with a 46 percent turnout rate among U.S.-born Hispanics. Among Asians, the turnout rate for naturalized immigrants was 49 percent, compared with 43 percent for the U.S. born."

53 Can immigrants become president?

The U.S. Constitution states, "No Person except a natural born Citizen ... shall be eligible to the Office of President." This includes people born outside the United States to American citizens.

54 Do American Indians have U.S. citizenship?

The Indian Citizenship Act of 1924 granted citizenship to Native Americans born in the United States. Members of the more than 560 federally recognized Indian tribes are also citizens of their tribal nations. These nations have sovereign rights of self government.

55 Are Puerto Ricans U.S. citizens?

Yes. Puerto Rico is one of 16 U.S. territories where people are citizens at birth. The United Nations considers Puerto Rico to be an independent nation, and there have been several votes on the island about its status. But the United States still considers people born there to be natural-born U.S. citizens. Some other U.S. territories are Guam, the U.S. Virgin Islands and the Northern Mariana Islands.

56 How has the U.S. policy change toward Cuba affected immigration?

In the 1960s, the United States began a program to grant Cuban immigrants refugee status and benefits. Once reaching a port of entry, they are allowed to stay after an inspection, which includes criminal and immigration history checks. After a year in the United States, they may apply for legal permanent residence. When Obama announced in 2014 that he would re-establish ties between the countries, Cubans worried the program would end. Immigration increased. According to U.S. Customs and Border Protection, it rose 78 percent from 24,278 in fiscal year 2014 to 43,159 in fiscal year 2015.

Shue-Qa Moua's father and mother emigrated from Laos to Thailand and then to the U.S. in 1976. Shue-Qa was born in California. View video at: http://immigrants.mndigital.org/items/show/512

Acceptance

57 Can states exclude immigrants?

No, states cannot exclude immigrants. Any attempt to do so would violate the U.S. Constitution and numerous federal and state civil rights laws. A 1941 ruling in Hines v. Davidowitz said, "the supremacy of national power in the field of foreign affairs and power over immigration/ naturalization/ deportation" is stipulated in the Constitution. It says states cannot override the federal government. The 2012 ruling in U.S. v. Arizona stands for the proposition that states may not enact immigration laws.

58 Are immigrants from all countries accepted equally?

No, and not all immigrants from the same country are treated alike. Immigrants arrive with different races, religions, languages and cultures. Each of those, regardless of country of origin, is met with different degrees of acceptance in the United States.

59 Do immigrants bring racial and social biases with them?

Of course, but one would not assume that everyone from one place thinks alike or that the biases there are the same as those in the United States. Depending on their experience, immigrants might be surprised by the prevalence of U.S. diversity or intolerance. Many immigrants find that Americans talk about race or assign it to people in different ways than they do in their home countries.

60 What are Americans' attitudes toward new immigrants?

In 2013, Public Opinion Quarterly summarized a number of major studies from 1992 to 2012. It found that negative feelings about immigrants rose after the 1994 election and the terror attacks of Sept. 11, 2001, followed by periods of more positive feelings. Generally, the report said, feelings improved since 2001 except in two areas: job competition and border enforcement. Support for deporting unauthorized immigrants was reported as having declined. The Southern Poverty Law Center said the number of anti-immigrant groups was up from 10 in 2014 to 12 in 2015.

61 How can U.S. citizens help immigrants feel more welcome?

U.S. Citizenship and Immigration Services gives grants to encourage such outreach. These are programs it has funded:

- Immigrant story-telling programs at libraries.
- Town hall meetings to promote integration as a two-way street.
- Partnerships with police to help immigrants set up neighborhood crime watches.
- Civics lessons with volunteer high school or college tutors.
- Talks at local coffee shops for practicing English conversation.

Nasser Mussa is ethnically Oromo and was born in Ethiopia, but grew up in Kenya. He came to Minnesota in 2005. View video at: http://immigrants.mndigital.org/items/show/502

Refugees and asylum seekers

62 What is the difference between refugees and asylum seekers?

These groups are defined under national and international laws. According to the United Nations, a refugee "is someone who has been forced to flee his or her country because of persecution, war, or violence. A refugee has a well-founded fear of persecution for reasons of race, religion, nationality, political opinion or membership in a particular social group." An asylum-seeker "is someone whose request for sanctuary has yet to be processed." The United States limits the number of refugees that may be admitted into the country. It is set by the president in consultation with Congress. There is no cap on the number of asylum seekers, but they must apply for asylum within a year of entering the United States.

63 What is refugee resettlement?

This is the settlement of refugees into an asylum country that has agreed to ultimately grant them permanent residence. Refugees must often wait for resettlement in an interim country. Some people have been born in and grow up in refugee camps. Refugees do not get to dictate the country where they will get asylum. In the United States, the Office of Refugee Resettlement works with the Department of Homeland Security and the State Department to make this happen.

64 What role do churches play in refugee resettlement?

Churches often provide sanctuary or sponsorship for immigrants and refugees seeking a safe living environment. Churches help with English and other training, jobs, housing, furnishings, transportation and emotional support. They might also assist with asylum claims or hearings.

65 Are U.S. citizens becoming more receptive to refugees?

Not really. Since the 1950s, studies by different organizations have shown that many Americans are not comfortable with refugees. Generally, they cite safety reasons. The Gallup polling company found that most Americans opposed resettlement of Hungarians in 1958. CBS/New York Times polling found opposition to Indochinese in 1979 and Cubans in 1980. A Bloomberg poll in 2015 found opposition to accepting Syrians. Still, the federal government admits refugees based on humanitarian reasons.

Wise Ali was born in Mogadishu, Somalia, in 1989. His family left Somalia in 1991 to escape the civil war. He moved to Kenya and lived there for 21 years in refugee camps. View video at: http://immigrants. mndigital.org/items/show/596

Unauthorized immigrants

66 Why is the term "unauthorized immigrant" preferred over "illegal alien" or "undocumented immigrant"?

Language, like immigration laws, changes. Language has moved away from indicating people are illegal. Actions are illegal, but people are not. "Illegals" is discouraged, too. There are other problems. People who came into the country on legal visas and who overstayed or who were brought in as children did not enter illegally, so unauthorized is more accurate. Unauthorized is more specific than undocumented. The word "alien" has one connotation in immigration law, but several derogatory ones, as well. In the 1970s, some Mexican-Americans argued for "illegal aliens" because it was less offensive than other terms then in use. U.S. Rep. Joaquín Castro, D-Texas, proposed in 2015 that the federal government no longer refer to immigrants as "aliens" and "illegal aliens." House Republicans have blocked the change, according to NBC News.

67 How many unauthorized immigrants are there in the United States?

According to New York's Center for Migration Studies, that number fell below 11 million in 2015, the lowest since 2003. The change was driven by a decline in the numbers of people from Mexico.

68 Do most unauthorized immigrants sneak in?

A 2016 Pew study found almost half the unauthorized immigrants in the United States did not sneak in. They entered with legal paperwork and did not leave when they were supposed to. They landed at airports or crossed at immigration checkpoints with temporary visas or Border Crossing Cards. Those allow short visits in the area around the border region. When people do not leave as they are supposed to, they are said to have overstayed or are called visa abusers. A little more than half of the unauthorized immigrants hid in vehicles such as cargo trucks or ships, or walked across the border from Mexico or Canada.

69 What does it mean to overstay?

A person who enters the country on a temporary visa, such as for school, travel or work, and who does not leave when they are supposed to is said to have overstayed. The Department of Homeland Security made its first estimate of overstays early in 2016. It said about 416,500 people out of 45 million who came into the country on temporary visas in 2015 overstayed. The largest group, 19 percent, were from Canada.

70 How do legal immigrants feel about those who come in illegally?

New America Media conducted the first such multilingual poll in 2006. It found "little resentment toward undocumented immigrants" by legal immigrants. The poll showed most legal immigrants agreed that unauthorized immigrants "take jobs that legal residents and citizens do not want to do" and "help the economy by providing low-cost labor." Legal immigrants, however, were concerned that anti-immigrant sentiment was hurting their families. In 2013, Pew asked 5,103 U.S. Hispanics about their views of unauthorized immigration. Fifty-three percent of Hispanic immigrants said that unauthorized immigrants had a positive impact on the U.S. Hispanic community. For U.S.-born Hispanics, the percentage with positive feelings was 35 percent. Both rankings were higher than those in a 2010 study.

71 Can unauthorized immigrants obtain driver's licenses?

Twelve states (California, Colorado, Connecticut, Delaware, Hawaii, Illinois, Maryland, Nevada, New Mexico, Utah, Vermont and Washington) and the District of Columbia permit unauthorized immigrants to obtain driver's licenses. Applicants must provide documents such as a foreign passport and proof of state residency.

Irma Márquez Trapero was born and raised in Culiacán, Sinaloa, Mexico. She arrived in St. James, Minnesota, in 1999 at the age of 9 with her parents and brother. They stayed with an uncle and intended to stay only temporarily. View video at: http://immigrants.mndigital.org/items/show/482

Deportation

72 What is the difference between deportation and detention?

Deportation means being removed from the country. Detention means being held, perhaps in advance of deportation, or after arriving. Immigrants who arrive in the United States and who are awaiting decisions on their status may be held at one of 200 detention centers. U.S. Immigration and Customs Enforcement oversees the program. It contracts for space with local jails and private prison companies. According to Detention Watch, the federal government detained 441,000 people in 2013. Some are held for years awaiting decisions.

73 Can people be deported if they are in the United States illegally?

If someone is found to be in the country illegally, they can be deported. A deportation ruling by an immigration court judge is required. Potential deportees have a right to appeal. Deportation orders are carried out by U.S. Immigration and Customs Enforcement. Deportees may apply for legal admission into the United States.

74 What happens when someone is deported?

Once deportation is ordered, a person usually has some time while travel documents and transportation are arranged. Once arranged, a letter will tell the deportee when and where to report and how much baggage may be brought. In other circumstances, a person may be arrested unannounced and taken back to their home country. The United States pays for deportations. Voluntary departures allow people to leave at their own expense. In these cases, their files do not reflect the deportation order, which could impede applications for visas or other legal immigration permits.

75 Can immigrants be deported after they become citizens?

U.S. citizens cannot be deported. However, the government might revoke a naturalized American's citizenship. This is called denaturalization. It is pursued in court for people who misrepresented themselves or did not disclose criminal histories when they applied for citizenship. Immigrants who lose their citizenship can be deported.

76 Can some members of a family get deported while others stay?

In a mixed-status family, unauthorized immigrant parents can be deported while their American citizen children may stay. The 2014 Deferred Action for Parents of Americans program was meant to address that. However, in 2016 on a 4-4 vote in U.S. v. Texas, the U.S. Supreme Court let stand a Texas federal district court's injunction stopping the program.

77 Is it true that the Obama administration deported more people than any other?

Yes. Despite promoting plans to allow unauthorized immigrants to stay and work, the Obama administration deported more than 2.5 million people. That is more than were deported from 1892-2000, according to Department of Homeland Security statistics. Deportations were heaviest in Obama's second term, driven by a 2014 crisis of people fleeing Central America. Deportation raids focused on people from those countries. Immigration advocates have complained that the United States is deporting people fleeing violence in Central America while supporting those fleeing violence in Syria. The Washington Post reported that "Administration officials fear that a failure to enforce the deportation orders against the Central American families would undermine their legal rationale for the deferred action program, which is based on the concept of 'prosecutorial discretion.'"

Families

78 Who are unaccompanied minors and border children?

These are children under 18 who make it into the country on their own without legal immigration status, parents or guardians. In recent years, thousands have come, fleeing gangs and drug violence in South and Central America. Many have died on the journey. Border children are put in the custody of the Office of Refugee Resettlement. They can either be placed with a family or deported. Traffic fluctuates because of changing conditions in the countries of origin and U.S. border enforcement. According to the Department of Homeland Security, apprehensions of unaccompanied children rose from 4,182 in July, 2015 to 6,775 that December. The number was 3,113 in February 2016.

79 What is a DREAMer?

The Development, Relief, and Education for Alien Minors Act, or DREAM Act, was first proposed in Congress in 2001. To date, it has not been approved. It would be a way for unauthorized immigrants to achieve conditional residency and, eventually, permanent residency. Its requirements are proof of having entered the country before age 16 and

continuous residence for at least five years; a high
school diploma or GED; good moral character and
passing criminal background checks.

80 Can people become citizens by marrying Americans?

Yes, but it is not easy. There are several steps and
much depends on each person's legal status. If one of
the parties is living overseas, they may have to stay
there during the process, which includes applications
and interviews, to make sure the marriage is
legitimate. Penalties for marriage fraud include up to
five years in prison and fines of as much as $250,000.
Other penalties are possible, especially for those who
arrange marriage conspiracies.

81 Do children become citizens if their parents naturalize?

This can happen automatically if the child is
under 18. The same is true for children from other
countries adopted by U.S. citizens.

82 If a non-citizen has a baby in the United States, is that baby a citizen?

Anyone born in the United States is automatically a
citizen. Babies born to American citizens outside the
United States are also U.S. citizens.

83 Do pregnant women come to the U.S. to have their babies born as citizens?

The derogatory term "anchor baby" was used in the 2016 presidential campaign to refer to babies born on U.S. soil to non-citizens. The "anchor" idea was that parents would then use their children's status to seek citizenship for themselves. Women have posed as tourists or obtained temporary visas that allowed them enough time to have their children in the United States. According to the Los Angeles Times, about "40,000 of the 300,000 children born to foreign citizens in the United States each year are the product of birth tourism." The Pew Research Center said there are organizations that bring unauthorized women into the United States to have children. Pew reported that 295,000 babies were born to unauthorized-immigrant parents in 2013, about 8 percent of U.S. births. This was down from 370,000 in 2007.

William Nyang'un, the youngest of five children, was born in Kenya in 1990. His mother moved to the United States when he was 6 months old, leaving him in the care of his family. He was reunited with them in the United States in 2012. View video at: http://immigrants.mndigital. org/items/show/575

Work and money

84 Do immigrants take jobs from Americans?

Usually not. Immigrants are hired for jobs that Americans don't want to do, can't do, or where the pay is low, causing a labor shortage. Citizens, especially lower income workers, have said in various studies that they must compete with immigrants for jobs. The idea is used in political campaigns. The Annenberg Public Policy Center's FactCheck.org says, "Study after study has shown that immigrants grow the economy, expanding demand for goods and services that the foreign-born workers and their families consume, thereby creating jobs. There is even broad agreement among economists that while immigrants may push down wages for some, the overall effect is to increase average wages for American-born workers."

85 How do immigrants contribute to the economy?

A major study on this was underway at The National Academies of Sciences, Engineering, and Medicine as this guide went to press. The previous major study was in 1997 by the National Academies of Science. It estimated that immigrants added about $10 billion a year to the U.S. economy. It said, "Immigration benefits the U.S. economy overall and has little negative effect on the income and job opportunities of most native-born Americans. Only in areas with high concentrations of low-skilled, low-paid immigrants are state and local taxpayers paying more on average to support the publicly funded services that these immigrants use."

86 Do unauthorized immigrants pay taxes?

Even unauthorized immigrants pay property, sales, gasoline, income, payroll and other taxes. It is estimated they pay around $13 billion a year in Social Security taxes, although they will not be eligible for those benefits. Other taxes are also deducted from their paychecks. The Institute on Taxation & Economic Policy estimated that unauthorized immigrants paid $11.8 billion in state and local taxes in 2012.

87 Why do immigrants dominate certain kinds of work?

U.S. immigration policy tilts toward people who work in high-demand fields such as information technology, engineering and medicine. From 1980 to 2010, the percentage of high-skilled immigrants increased, while low-skilled immigrants declined.

In 2014, according to the Migration Policy Institute, immigrants accounted for 16 percent of U.S. workers. Concentrations were higher in computer programming at 32 percent, health-care support professionals at 30 percent, and physicians at 26 percent. On the local level, concentrations of workers from one nationality occur. Local examples include cabbies, truck drivers and nail salon workers. Networking, migration of families and micro loans can contribute to this. This can also occur nationally. One example is that immigrants from India own or operate about half the motels in the United States. About a third of immigrants over age 25 who lack high school diplomas work in the hotel and restaurant industries, which do not require skilled labor and pay lower wages.

88 Do employers recruit immigrants?

Some employers are very active in this. Faced with a shortage of qualified workers or looking to pay lower wages, employers seek immigrant workers. The Immigration Reform and Control Act of 1986 says that employers may not discriminate against noncitizens who have work authorization.

89 Do immigrants start businesses?

Approximately 10 percent of immigrants start businesses, which is about double that of non-immigrants. A report by Partnership for a New American Economy reported that 90 of the Fortune 500 companies had been founded by immigrants and 114 others had been founded by children of immigrants. CNN reports that 70 percent of the world's most valuable brands come from American companies founded by immigrants. Immigrants founded AT&T, Google, Yahoo, Kohl's, Nordstrom, Colgate, Sara Lee and Kraft Foods.

90 Can immigrants get financial credit, loans and mortgages?

Immigrants can have challenges with this because they don't have U.S. credit histories. Getting loans and credit is easier after someone has worked in the United States and established a tax and financial credit history.

91 Can non-citizens join the U.S. military?

They may if they are legal permanent residents. Many non-citizens fought for the United States in Iraq and Afghanistan. Serving in the military does not guarantee citizenship, though naturalization requirements may be diminished or waived for veterans. From 2002 to 2015, 109,000 U.S. service members became citizens.

92 What is a deported veteran?

Non-citizen veterans who commit crimes after returning to civilian life may have their green cards revoked and be deported. Banished Veterans and lawyers who work with this advocacy group estimate there are hundreds or thousands of deported veterans.

93 How much welfare do unauthorized immigrants use?

Unauthorized immigrants are not eligible for welfare, food stamps, Medicaid or most public benefits. Since 1996, welfare law has required legal immigrants to be in the United States for at least five years to receive these benefits.

94 Do immigrants send money out of the country?

Many do. Some come to the United States to help earn money for their families. These payments are called remittances. To send them, people must prove they are legal immigrants. Unauthorized immigrants cannot legally send money to their home countries. For legal immigrants and expatriates, there are various international fund transfer rules and high fees for remittances. The Bureau of Economic Analysis estimated that $40 billion in remittances were sent out of the United States by immigrant wage earners in 2014. However, the U.S. General

Accountability Office questioned the accuracy of the estimate and asked for more research.

95 Do immigrants contribute to the crime rate?

Crime records indicate there is not a link between immigration and criminal behavior. According to the American Immigration Council, immigrants are five times less likely than the nonimmigrant population to be incarcerated. The 2010 American Community Survey reported that the incarceration rate for men 18-39, the largest share of the U.S. prison population, was 3.3 percent for native-born men and slightly less than half of that for immigrant males in that age group.

96 Is it rude to assume or ask if someone is a U.S. citizen?

It can be. It might imply that someone doesn't belong or fit in. It can be like asking someone from the United States, "What country are you from?" Appearance and speech will not tell you. If people tell you they are immigrants and you already know them somewhat, you might talk about their citizenship, but don't assume or make it the first or only question in learning about them.

Natasha Gomez, daughter of a Colombian immigrant who served with the U.S. Navy in Japan, has a flexible identity tied to Spanish, Japanese and English. View video at: http://immigrants.mndigital.org/items/show/572

Education

97 What do we know about the educational levels of adult immigrants?

From 1990 to 2000, the number of immigrants with college educations increased 89 percent, while the number of native-born citizens with college degrees rose 32 percent. From 2000 to 2014, the number of immigrants with degrees went up another 78 percent, and the number of native-born citizens with degrees went up 39 percent. According to the Migration Policy Institute, from 1990 to 2014, the proportion of all degree holders in the United States who were immigrants rose from 10 percent to 16 percent.

98 Are overseas diplomas accepted in U.S. job markets?

This depends on where the diploma was earned and in which field. More than 50 professions have certification and similar requirements in the United States. They include medicine, accounting and dentistry. To work in the United States in these fields, credentials must be verified by either the Association of International Evaluators or the National

Association of Credential Evaluation Services. There is a fee for verification, and educational qualifications are only one part of licensing. Immigrant professionals may work in alternative jobs until they become recertified in their fields.

99 Can children of unauthorized immigrants attend U.S. public schools?

The 1982 U.S. Supreme Court case Plyer v. Doe ruled that unauthorized immigrant children "have the same right to attend public primary and secondary schools as do U.S. citizens and permanent residents." States mandate that immigrant children attend school until the age required for children who are citizens. Public schools may not deny admission to students or treat students any differently based on immigration status.

100 What challenges do immigrant children face in school?

There are several. First, if they are not fluent in English, it may be more difficult to fit into the classroom and social environment. Second, a different culture and clothing style can make any child a target for bullying. Third, their home culture is not being taught in American schools, therefore, they could have trouble transitioning between cultures.

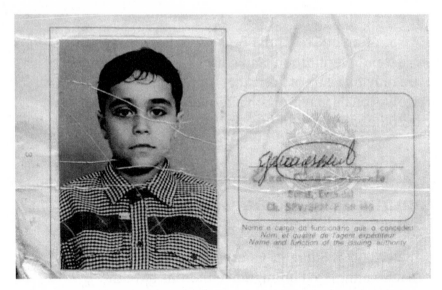

Thiago Heilman was born in Brazil in 1984. In April 1996, his family came to New York City and he stayed in the United States to continue his education after the rest of his family returned to Brazil. View video at: http://immigrants.mndigital.org/items/show/573

Do you know enough to be a citizen?

One of the steps to becoming a citizen is to answer 10 questions about U.S. government, history and civics chosen from a battery of 100. Questions are provided by U.S. Citizen and Immigrant Services. How can you do with these 10 items from the battery?

1. How many amendments does the Constitution have?
2. The House of Representatives has how many voting members?
3. If both the president and the vice president can no longer serve, who becomes president?
4. Name one right only for United States citizens.
5. What is one reason colonists came to America?
6. The Federalist Papers supported the passage of the U.S. Constitution. Name one of the writers.

7. What territory did the United States buy from France in 1803?

8. Who was president during the Great Depression and World War II?

9. Name one U.S. territory.

10. What is the name of the national anthem?

To become a citizen, you need to get six right. Would you pass? See page 65 to find out.

These are the answers the U.S. Citizen and Immigrant Services suggests. Some items have additional correct answers.

1. Twenty-seven (27)
2. Four hundred thirty-five (435)
3. The speaker of the House
4. Vote in a federal election or run for federal office
5. Suggested answers are freedom, political liberty, religious freedom, economic opportunity, practice their religion, escape persecution.
6. Correct answers are (James) Madison, (Alexander) Hamilton, (John) Jay and Publius
7. The Louisiana Territory or Louisiana
8. (Franklin) Roosevelt
9. Correct answers include Puerto Rico, U.S. Virgin Islands, American Samoa, Northern Mariana Islands and Guam.
10. The Star-Spangled Banner

How did you do?

Resources

Arnold, Kathleen R. *Anti-Immigration in the United States: A Historical Encyclopedia* (two volumes). Santa Barbara: Greenwood, 2011. Print.

Chomsky, Aviva. *They Take Our Jobs! and 20 Other Myths About Immigration.* Boston: Beacon Press, 2007. Print.

Ciment, James and John Radzilowski, editors. *American Immigration: An Encyclopedia of Political, Social and Cultural Change* (four volumes), second edition. Armonk: Sharpe Reference, 2014. Print.

Eaton, Susan E. *Integration Nation: Immigrants, Refugees, and America at its Best.* New York: The New Press, 2016 Print.

Ghadar, Fariborz. *Becoming American: Why Immigration is Good for Our Nation's Future.* New York: Rowman & Littlefield, 2014. Print.

Gonzalez, Juan. *Harvest of Empire: A History of Latinos in America.* New York: Penguin Books, 2000. Print

Gonzalez, Roberto G. *Lives in Limbo: Undocumented and Coming of Age in America.* Oakland: University of California Press, 2015. Print.

Len-Rios, M.E., and Ernest Perry, E. *Who is an American? Cross-Cultural Journalism.* New York: Routledge, 2016. Print.

Truax, Eileen. *Dreamers: An Immigrant Generation's Fight for Their American Dream.* Boston: Beacon Press, 2015. Print.

Yoshikawa, Hirokazu. *Immigrants Raising Children: Undocumented Parents and Their Children.* New York: Russell Sage Foundation, 2012. Print.

U.S. government

Centers for Disease Control and Prevention

http://www.cdc.gov/

Department of Homeland Security

2013 Statistical Yearbook

http://www.dhs.gov/sites/default/files/publications/ois_yb_2013_0.pdf

Office of Immigration Statistics

http://www.dhs.gov/office-immigration-statistics

U.S. Bureau of Justice Statistics

http://www.bjs.gov/

U.S. Bureau of Labor Statistics

http://www.bls.gov/

U.S. Census Bureau

http://www.census.gov/

U.S. Census Bureau's American Fact Finder

http://factfinder.census.gov/

U.S. Citizenship and Immigration Services (part of the Department of Homeland Security)

https://my.uscis.gov/

U.S. Department of Education

http://www.ed.gov/

U.S. Department of Labor

https://www.dol.gov/

U.S. Department of State

http://travel.state.gov/content/travel/en.html

Organizations

American Civil Liberties Union

http://www.aclu.org

American Immigration Council

http://www.immigrationpolicy.org/

American Immigration Lawyers Association

http://www.aila.org

Gallup Immigration Report

http://www.gallup.com/poll/1660/immigration.aspx

Human Rights Watch

https://www.hrw.org/

Immigration and the States Project, Pew Charitable Trusts

http://www.pewtrusts.org/en/projects/
immigration-and-the-states-project

Institute for Immigration Research at George Mason University

http://iir.gmu.edu/about

Migration Policy Institute

http://www.migrationpolicy.org/

The National Academies of Sciences, Engineering, and Medicine

http://national academies.org

New America Media

http://newamericamedia.org/

Pew Research Center immigration page

http://www.pewresearch.org/topics/immigration

Robert Wood Johnson Foundation

http://www.rwjf.org/

Southern Poverty Law Center

https://www.splcenter.org

University of Minnesota's Immigration History Research Center

http://immigrants.mndigital.org/

The Wilson Center: Immigrants in the United States: How Well are They Integrating into Society?

https://www.wilsoncenter.org/sites/default/files/integration-Jimenez.pdf

Our Story

The 100 Questions and Answers series springs from the idea that good journalism should increase cross-cultural competence and understanding. Most of our guides are created by Michigan State University journalism students.

We use journalistic interviews to surface the simple, everyday questions that people have about each other but might be afraid to ask. We use research and reporting to get the answers and then put them where people can find them, read them and learn about each other.

These cultural competence guides are meant to be conversation starters. We want people to use these guides to get some baseline understanding and to feel comfortable asking more questions. We put a resources section in every guide we make and we arrange community conversations. While the guides can answer questions in private, they are meant to spark discussions.

Making these has taught us that people are not that different from each other. People share more similarities than differences. We all want the same things for ourselves and for our families. We want to be accepted, respected and understood.

Please email your thoughts and suggestions to Series Editor Joe Grimm at joe.grimm@gmail.com, at the Michigan State University School of Journalism.

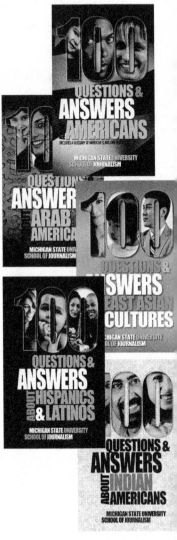

http://news.jrn.msu.edu/culturalcompetence

Related Books

100 Questions and Answers About Americans
Michigan State University School of Journalism, 2013
This guide answers some of the first questions asked by newcomers to the United States. Questions represent dozens of nationalities coming from Africa, Asia, Australia, Europe and North and South America. Good for international students, guests and new immigrants.
http://news.jrn.msu.edu/culturalcompetence/

ISBN: 978-1-939880-20-8

100 Questions and Answers About Arab Americans
Michigan State University School of Journalism, 2014
The terror attacks of Sept. 11, 2001, propelled these Americans into a difficult position where they are victimized twice. The guide addresses stereotypes, bias and misinformation. Key subjects are origins, religion, language and customs. A map shows places of national origin.
http://news.jrn.msu.edu/culturalcompetence/

ISBN: 978-1-939880-56-7

100 Questions and Answers About East Asian Cultures
Michigan State University School of Journalism, 2014
Large university enrollments from Asia prompted this guide as an aid for understanding cultural differences. The focus is on people from China, Japan, Korea and Taiwan and includes Mongolia, Hong Kong and Macau. The guide includes history, language, values, religion, foods and more.
http://news.jrn.msu.edu/culturalcompetence/

ISBN: 978-939880-50-5

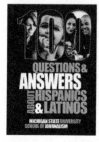

100 Questions and Answers About Hispanics & Latinos
Michigan State University School of Journalism, 2014
This group became the largest ethnic minority in the United States in 2014 and this guide answers many of the basic questions about it. Questions were suggested by Hispanics and Latinos. Includes maps and charts on origin and size of various Hispanic populations.
http://news.jrn.msu.edu/culturalcompetence/

ISBN: 978-1-939880-44-4

Print and ebooks available from Amazon.com and other retailers.

Related Books

100 Questions and Answers About Indian Americans
Michigan State University School of Journalism, 2013
In answering questions about Indian Americans, this guide also addresses Pakistanis, Bangladeshis and others from South Asia. The guide covers religion, issues of history, colonization and national partitioning, offshoring and immigration, income, education, language and family.
http://news.jrn.msu.edu/culturalcompetence/

ISBN: 978-1-939880-00-0 m

100 Questions, 500 Nations: A Guide to Native America
Michigan State University School of Journalism, 2014
This guide was created in partnership with the Native American Journalists Association. The guide covers tribal sovereignty, treaties and gaming, in addition to answers about population, religion, U.S. policies and politics. The guide includes the list of federally recognized tribes.
http://news.jrn.msu.edu/culturalcompetence/

ISBN: 978-1-939880-38-3

100 Questions and Answers About Veterans
Michigan State University School of Journalism, 2015
This guide treats the more than 20 million U.S. military veterans as a cultural group with distinctive training, experiences and jargon. Graphics depict attitudes, adjustment challenges, rank, income and demographics. Includes six video interviews by Detroit Public Television.
http://news.jrn.msu.edu/culturalcompetence/

ISBN: 978-1-942011-00-2

100 Questions and Answers About American Jews
We begin by asking and answering what it means to be Jewish in America. The answers to these wide-ranging, base-level questions will ground most people and set them up for meaningful conversations with Jewish acquaintances. We cover matters of faith, food, culture, politics and stereotypes.
http://news.jrn.msu.edu/culturalcompetence/

ISBN: 978-1-942011-22-4

Print and ebooks available from Amazon.com and other retailers.

Related Books

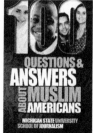

100 Questions and Answers About Muslim Americans
Michigan State University School of Journalism, 2014
This guide was done at a time of rising intolerance in the United States toward Muslims. The guide describes the presence of this religious group around the world and inside the United States. It includes audio on how to pronounce some basic Muslim words.
http://news.jrn.msu.edu/culturalcompetence/

ISBN: 978-1-939880-79-6

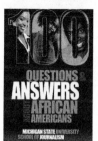

100 Questions and Answers About African Americans
Michigan State University School of Journalism, 2016
Learn about the racial issues that W.E.B. DuBois said in 1900 would be the big challenge for the 20th century. This guide explores Black and African American identity, history, language, contributions and more. Learn more about current issues in American cities and campuses.
http://news.jrn.msu.edu/culturalcompetence/

ISBN: 978-1-942011-19-4

To My Professor
"To My Professor: Student Voices for Great College Teaching" begins with remarks by students about their professors. They tend not to be the kind of remarks that professors usually hear, and some are harsh. Teaching college is difficult and this book has some potential solutions. More than 50 chapters cover situations including expectations, communication, technology, race, gender and religion, mental and physical health.

ISBN: 978-1-942011-49-1

THE NEW BULLYING
Bullying has changed considerably. This book is intended to document that change. Among the changes that were examined are the rise of cyberbullying, social exclusion as a form of bullying, new laws about school bullying, computer crimes and threats and a growing willingness on the part of the public to talk about bullying and its perceived connection to suicide and violence, especially in schools.

ISBN: 978-1-934879-63-4

Print and ebooks available from Amazon.com and other retailers.

CPSIA information can be obtained at www.ICGtesting.com
Printed in the USA
BVOW08s1405290916

463474BV00011B/6/P